Soccer

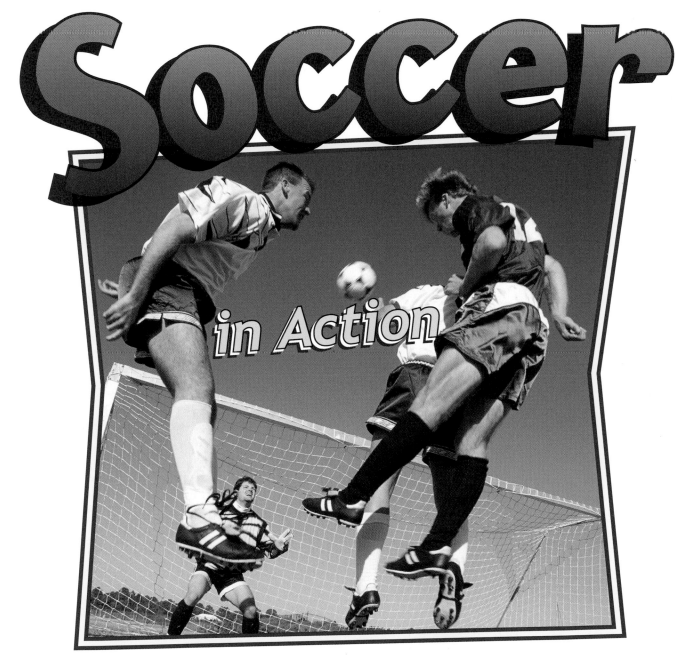

in Action

Niki Walker & Sarah Dann

Crabtree Publishing Company

Created by Bobbie Kalman

To Dylan, Myles, & Tess Turner
with cheers from the sidelines

Editor-in-Chief
Bobbie Kalman

Writing team
Niki Walker
Sarah Dann
John Crossingham

Managing editor
Lynda Hale

Editors
Kate Calder
Jane Lewis

Computer design
Lynda Hale
Niki Walker
Robert MacGregor (cover concept)

Consultant
Len Turton is a founder of
St. Catharines' youth soccer
and a longtime soccer coach.

Special thanks to
Andrew Corolis, Nikolai Coutinho, Christina Gittings, Ransom Hawley,
Sarah McNally, Danielle Paolone, Akshay Shetty, Anne Kubu, Paul Lewis,
and Ridley College; Mr. John Childs, Mrs. Kajak, Ms. Ricciardelli, Shawn
Knott, Tran Duy Binh, Akins Fortune, Kristi Evenden, Lydia Zemaitis, Kelsey
Westbrook, Michael Zigomanis, Kyle Derry, Neil Bell, Ali Raza, Fatima Ahmed,
Holly Morin, Rachel Ward, Abby Hume, and Earl Haig Public School;
Linda Weigl and Warren Rylands; Sam Turton; Josh Wiwcharyk

Photographs
Marc Crabtree: pages 13, 19, 20, 21 (both), 23, 24, 27, 28 (top), 29 (both); Bruce
Curtis: pages 12, 16, 17, 18, 28 (bottom), 30 (bottom); Bob Tringali/SportsChrome:
page 22; Linda Weigl: page 14; other images by Digital Stock and Eyewire, Inc.

Illustrations
Trevor Morgan: soccer balls throughout book, pages 4, 6-7, 9, 12, 13
Bonna Rouse: pages 10-11, 15, 17, 19, 22, 23, 25, 26, 27, 31 (bottom)

Production coordinator
Hannelore Sotzek

Digital prepress
Embassy Graphics

Crabtree Publishing Company

PMB 16A
350 Fifth Avenue,
Suite 3308
New York, NY
10118

360 York Road
RR 4
Niagara-on-the-Lake,
Ontario, Canada
L0S 1J0

73 Lime Walk
Headington,
Oxford
OX3 7AD
United Kingdom

Cataloging in Publication Data
Walker, Niki
    Soccer in action

(Sports in action)
Includes index.

ISBN 0-7787-0161-1 (library bound) ISBN 0-7787-0173-5 (pbk.)
This book introduces the techniques, equipment, rules, and safety
requirements of soccer.

1. Soccer—Juvenile literature. 2. Soccer—Training—Juvenile literature.
[1. Soccer.] I. Dann, Sarah, 1970- . II. Title. III. Series: Kalman, Bobbie.
Sports in action.

GV943.25.W35 2000   j796.334   LC 99-38040
                                                              CIP

Contents

What is Soccer?

Soccer is the most popular sport in the world. People love it because it is fast-paced and exciting. Players on two teams run up and down a field trying to score **goals** by sending the ball into their opponents' net. The team with the highest score wins. Only the **goalkeepers** are allowed to touch the ball with their hands. The other players can touch the ball with only their legs, feet, chest, and head. Most soccer games, or **matches**, are 90 minutes long. In most countries outside North America, soccer is called **football**.

Worldwide competition

More than 150 countries belong to the worldwide organization called **Fédération Internationale de Football Associations**, or **FIFA**. FIFA organizes international soccer competitions.

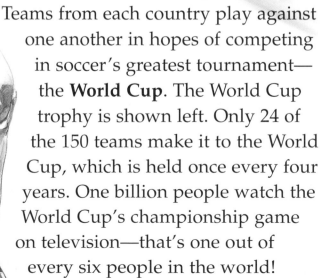

Teams from each country play against one another in hopes of competing in soccer's greatest tournament— the **World Cup**. The World Cup trophy is shown left. Only 24 of the 150 teams make it to the World Cup, which is held once every four years. One billion people watch the World Cup's championship game on television—that's one out of every six people in the world!

Welcome to the Pitch

Soccer games are played on a large, rectangular field called a **pitch**. The pitch is marked with lines, as shown in the diagram below. There are eleven players on a soccer team. Each member of the team plays a different **position**, which means he or she covers a certain area of the pitch.

A soccer game begins with a **kickoff**. The ball is placed on the **center spot**, and a member of the starting team makes a short forward pass to a teammate. Opponents are not allowed in the center circle until the ball has been touched. A kickoff also takes place after a goal is scored and at the start of the second half.

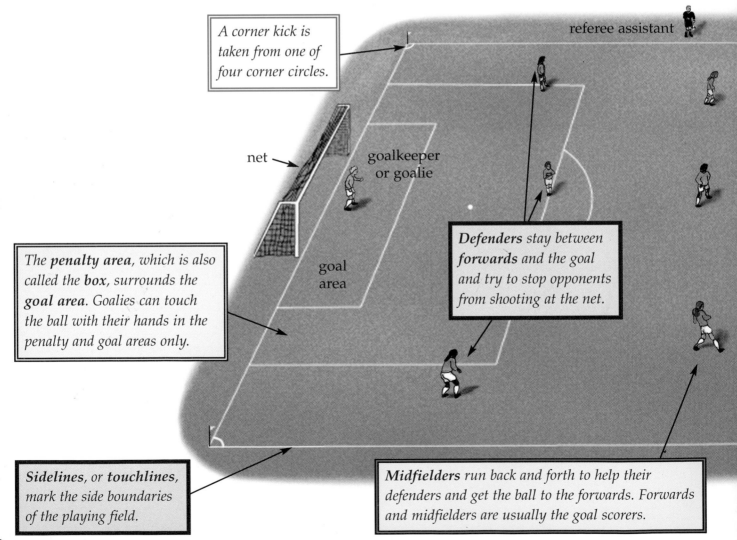

A corner kick is taken from one of four corner circles.

referee assistant

net

goalkeeper or goalie

goal area

The **penalty area**, which is also called the **box**, surrounds the **goal area**. Goalies can touch the ball with their hands in the penalty and goal areas only.

Defenders stay between **forwards** and the goal and try to stop opponents from shooting at the net.

Sidelines, or **touchlines**, mark the side boundaries of the playing field.

Midfielders run back and forth to help their defenders and get the ball to the forwards. Forwards and midfielders are usually the goal scorers.

Attacking and defending

A team plays **offense** or **defense**, depending on whether or not it has the ball. In the diagram below, the red team has the ball, so it is playing offense, or **attacking**. Its players try to score. The blue team is on defense. Its players try to get back the ball and stop the other team from scoring. Players must be ready to switch quickly between attacking and defending.

Out-of-bounds

Players sometimes send the ball **out-of-bounds**. If you send the ball over the sideline, the other team gets to throw in the ball from the point where the ball went out. If you put the ball past the opposing team's goal line, the goalkeeper kicks the ball back into play. If you send the ball past your own goal line, the opposing team gets a **corner kick** to put the ball back into play.

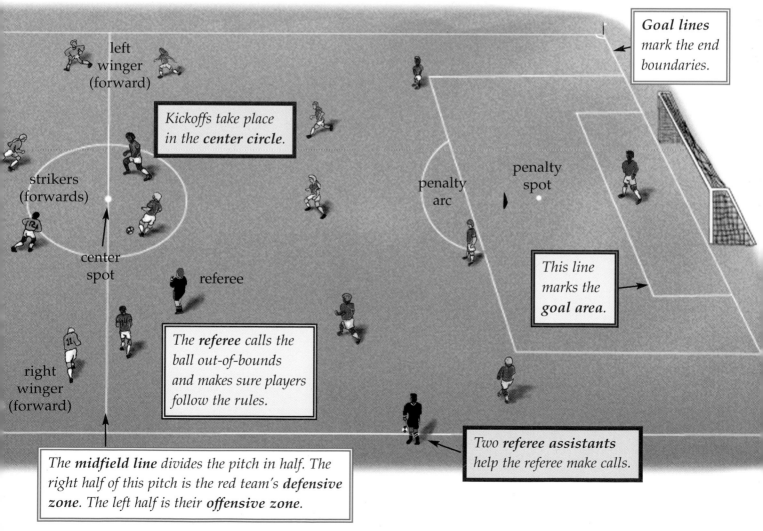

left winger (forward)

*Kickoffs take place in the **center circle**.*

Goal lines mark the end boundaries.

strikers (forwards)

penalty arc

penalty spot

center spot

referee

*This line marks the **goal area**.*

right winger (forward)

*The **referee** calls the ball out-of-bounds and makes sure players follow the rules.*

*Two **referee assistants** help the referee make calls.*

*The **midfield line** divides the pitch in half. The right half of this pitch is the red team's **defensive zone**. The left half is their **offensive zone**.*

The Essentials

Soccer does not require much equipment. A ball is all you need to practice skills and play games for fun. If you want to play in a **league**, however, you'll need the equipment described on the opposite page.

Suiting up

Team uniforms are made up of a lightweight shirt, a pair of shorts, and knee socks. Players wear **shin guards** under their socks. Proper footwear is also required.

Ready in goal

Goalies wear shorts or pants and a long-sleeved shirt. The goalie's shirt is a different color than those worn by the rest of the team, so it is easy to spot the goalie among the other players. Goalies sometimes wear a padded uniform. The padding protects them when they dive for the ball. Many goalies also wear gloves with grips to help them catch and hold the ball.

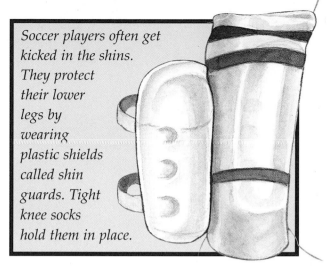

Soccer players often get kicked in the shins. They protect their lower legs by wearing plastic shields called shin guards. Tight knee socks hold them in place.

Soccer balls are made of leather. Balls come in three sizes: sizes 3 and 4 for children and size 5 for teenagers and adults.

*Lightweight shoes called **boots** help players kick the ball with control. There are plastic **cleats**, or studs, on the bottom of the boots. Cleats dig into the ground and give players a better grip as they run, stop, and change direction. Always wipe any mud from between the cleats after wearing them. Air out your shoes by loosening the laces and pulling up the tongue.*

A water bottle should be a standard part of your equipment. Exercise makes you sweat, and your body loses water. You can get sick if you don't stop for a drink, especially on hot days.

Warming Up

Before practicing or playing, it is important to stretch and warm up your muscles. Warming up loosens your muscles so you move better, and it helps prevent injuries such as muscle strains and pulls. Although you use mainly your legs when playing soccer, you still need to limber up the rest of your body. Move slowly and never bounce or stretch more than feels comfortable.

Trunk circles

Stand with your feet shoulder-width apart, and put your hands on your hips. Swing your hips in a circle, keeping your feet flat on the ground and your shoulders as still as possible.

Arm circles

Swing your arms in large circles. Keep making smaller circles until your arms are straight out to the side and moving in tiny circles. Reverse the direction, starting with small circles and ending with giant ones.

Neck stretch

It is easy to hurt your neck, so do this stretch carefully. Stand with your feet slightly apart. Tilt your head forward so that your chin points to your chest. Now slowly move your head toward one shoulder and then the other. Do not roll your head backward or more than feels comfortable. Do five stretches toward each shoulder.

Hamstring stretch

Stand on your left foot. Use your left hand to support yourself against a wall. Bring your right foot up behind you until you can grab it with your right hand. Pull gently until you feel the stretch in the front of your leg. Hold the stretch for a count of ten, then switch sides.

Ankle stretch

Sit on the ground with one leg straight. Bend your other leg so that you can grab your foot. Gently move it in circles. When you've done ten, stop and do ten circles in the other direction. Change legs.

Leg lunges

Stand with your feet wide apart. Bend your left knee until you feel a stretch in the inside of your right leg. Hold the stretch for a count of five. Straighten up and switch sides.

"V" stretch

Sit with your legs in a "V." Stretch your arms out in front of you until you feel a stretch in the back of your legs and buttocks. Hold the stretch for a count of ten.

Meet the Ball ⚽

Before you start practicing any soccer skills, you should get to know the ball. Learn how it moves when you kick it with different parts of your feet. Try kicking various spots on the ball and see what happens. Knowing how the ball moves will help you with skills such as passing and shooting. During a game, you will need to make long kicks down the field as well as short, tricky passes to get around an opponent.

To get a feel for the ball, knock it back and forth between your feet. Start slowly and gradually build up speed.

Using your boot

Every time you make a pass or shoot at the net, you must decide which part of your foot to use. Each part of your foot makes the ball move in a different way.

Kicking with the inside of your boot gives you the most power and accuracy.

You can use your heel to knock the ball a short distance behind you.

The outside of the boot is good for making tricky passes when an opponent is near.

The toe of your boot provides the least control over the ball.

Clowning around

One of the best ways to develop your coordination, reflexes, and ball-handling skills is **juggling**. When you juggle, you keep the ball in the air by bouncing it off your feet, knees, chest, and legs—no hands are allowed! See how many hits in a row you can get before losing control of the ball. To challenge yourself, try hitting the ball five times in a row with your feet, then five times with your knees, and so on.

This boy is practicing juggling. You can juggle by yourself, with a partner, or with a group of friends.

The key to aiming

Learning how to move the ball where you want it to go takes practice. Imagine that your ball has lines marked on it, as shown below, and aiming will become much easier.

Kick the top of the ball to make it bounce roughly along the ground.

Kick the ball where the lines cross, and you will make it roll straight ahead.

Kick the ball on the right side to move it to the left.

Kick the left side of the ball to send it to the right.

Kick the bottom half of the ball to send it high into the air.

Get Your Kicks ⚽

Kicking is the most important skill you need to be a good soccer player. You need to kick the ball quickly and accurately in order to make great passes and score goals. It sounds easy enough—just swing your leg and whack the ball with your foot, right? Wrong. Learn the different types of kicks described here and put them to use by practicing the drills on the following pages.

*While you kick, keep your head down and look at the ball—not the target. As long as your **support foot**, or non-kicking foot, is pointing at your target, the ball will go toward it. It is also important to keep the ankle of your kicking foot rigid when you kick the ball. Keeping your ankle rigid gives power to your kick.*

Airborne shot

For a long shot, kick the ball into the air. Put your support foot beside and a little behind the ball. With your **instep**, kick the ball just below its middle and **follow through**, or keep swinging your leg, after you connect with the ball.

Outside shot

An **outside shot** is for short, quick kicks and sideways passes. Put your support foot to the side and behind the ball. Kick the ball with the outside of your kicking foot and follow through.

Straight pass

A **straight pass** rolls the ball smoothly. Put your support foot beside the ball and kick with the inside of your other foot. Follow through.

Chip shot

Chipping sends the ball high into the air for a short distance. To chip, follow the directions for the airborne shot but do not follow through.

On the Move ⚽

Imagine that you have the ball in your end of the soccer pitch. An opponent is running toward you, and none of your teammates are open for a pass. What do you do? Get moving! You can't just run, though—you have to **dribble**, or move the ball with you. It seems easy enough—give the ball a little kick, take a step, another kick, and so on— but you must be able to do it at full speed and without looking down at the ball!

*This boy is keeping his head up as he dribbles the ball. By looking ahead, he can see teammates who are **open**, or available, for a pass and also avoid opponents.*

The basic dribble

Dribble the ball by tapping it back and forth between your feet. The ball travels in a zigzag pattern even though you move in a straight line. Tap the ball just hard enough so that, as you take each step, it is already there for you to kick. If the ball gets too far away from you, an opponent will zoom in and steal it.

These illustrations show how the ball crosses your path during a basic dribble.

Dribbling drill

Set up six markers in a row, each about three giant steps apart. Use anything for markers—shoes, t-shirts, or pylons. Dribble down the row, moving around each marker as quickly as you can without losing control of the ball. When you reach the end, turn around and dribble back to the starting point.

start

Fast and furious

When you feel comfortable with the basic dribble, try kicking the ball straight ahead of you instead of side to side. You don't have to switch feet with each kick—use whichever foot is closer to the ball. Also, practice kicking with the outside of your feet as you run. This dribble lets you run much faster than the basic dribble because the ball doesn't cross your path.

Kicking the ball straight ahead is useful when you have a lot of ground to cover and there are no opponents nearby.

Passing

Passing is an important skill to master. It is usually easier to pass the ball to a teammate than to try moving it around an opponent. Passing also moves the ball up the field more quickly than dribbling. It lets you get the ball to a teammate who is in position to score. It is easiest to practice passing by doing it with a friend. Pass the ball to each other. Stop it each time before you pass it back. The next step is to continue passing it back and forth without stopping the ball. If you don't have a partner, use a wall instead. It always sends the ball back right away!

The player who is about to kick the ball has two opponents nearby. By passing to an open teammate, he helps his team keep the ball.

Passing on the run

Get one or more friends together to practice passing while running. Spread out and run up the field, passing the ball to one another. Aim the ball and kick it hard enough so that no one has to slow down or stop and go back for it. When you kick the ball, aim for a spot slightly ahead of your receiver. The ball should reach a spot at the same time as the receiver and he or she can keep running full-speed toward the net.

Keep the ball rolling! After you make a pass to a teammate, don't stop and watch! Keep running ahead and be ready for a return pass.

Play monkey-in-the-middle with a group of friends. Form a circle around one player, or the "monkey." Players forming the circle try passing the ball to one another without letting the monkey get it. If the monkey stops the pass, he or she switches places with the passer.

Many times during a game, you will need to get control of a ball that is flying through the air or moving quickly along the ground. This skill is called **trapping**. When the ball is moving close to the ground, you can trap it with your foot. If it is bouncing higher, you can use almost any part of your body except your arms and hands. Get a friend to toss you a ball so you can practice trapping it.

Use your thigh to trap a ball moving just below your waist. Raise your leg off the ground so that the ball hits your thigh and rolls down. Notice how this player keeps his arms and hands as far from the ball as possible. He doesn't want to touch the ball with them by accident.

Set your trap

Whichever part of your body you use as a trap, such as your foot, chest, or leg, make sure it is relaxed. If your body is stiff, the ball will bounce away. As the ball hits you, move back slightly to cushion the impact. The ball will drop to the ground.

High-ball trapping

Trap high balls with your chest. If the ball is heading up from the ground, lean over it with your chest, as shown below. If the ball is on its way down, lean back to trap it, as shown left. A chest trap is the only time a female player other than the goalie can touch the ball with her arms.

(above) This player turns her palms inward so that she doesn't accidentally touch the ball with her hands.

# Heads Up!

When the ball is traveling too high to be trapped by your chest, you can still get control of it by jumping up and hitting it with your head. It sounds painful, but **heading** should not hurt when it is done properly. It is a necessary skill to master, because you can use it to surprise your opponents with a quick pass or shot.

*Hit the ball at your **hairline**, shown here by the blue spot.*

Try to keep your eyes open and your mouth closed—you need to see the ball if you're going to hit it, but if you hit it with your mouth open, you could bite your tongue. Ouch!

*Don't wait for the ball to hit you! It is important to move at the ball with your head. As the ball approaches, bend your knees and arch your back. When the ball is almost at your forehead, straighten your knees and back and **connect**, or make contact, with the ball.*

Easy does it

Hitting the ball with your head can be scary—after all, you don't want it to smash into your nose! Start practicing this skill with an inflatable beach ball. Hold it just above your head, let go, and gently tap it with your forehead. When you're comfortable bouncing the ball off your forehead, toss it into the air and head it as it falls. Push it in different directions with your forehead. When you feel ready, practice with a soccer ball.

Take your time learning to head the ball. Your skills will improve with practice.

Get a friend to toss the ball so you can head it back. As you improve, have your friend move farther away from you. You can also set up targets and practice your aim. When you and your friend are great headers, try heading the ball to each other without catching it or letting it touch the ground. If you want to practice alone, try heading a ball against a wall. See how many times you can hit it in a row.

Take Your Best Shot ⚽

Since the object of a soccer game is to score goals, shooting is a skill you should practice as much as possible. Soccer nets may be big, but goalies know how to guard them well. You have to find an open spot to shoot at, and you have to know how to kick the ball so it travels under, around, or over the goalie and other defenders.

When you're first learning to shoot, place the ball on the ground and practice kicking it properly (see pages 14-15). As you improve, try running toward the ball before you shoot it. Take short, quick steps as you move toward the ball. Taking short strides makes it easier to get your support foot in the correct position, which gives power to your kick.

Pick a spot on the net or mark a target on a wall with chalk. Practice hitting your target using each foot. When you hit your target five times in a row, move back two steps and start again.

Aim's the game

Practice, practice, practice your aim first, and worry about the power of your shots later. It doesn't matter how hard you can kick the ball if you can't direct it toward your target!

Shooting on the fly

You won't have time to stop the ball before you shoot it at the net. During a game, you will have to keep running as you make a shot. To practice shooting while moving, get a friend to roll or toss the ball toward you as you run. Practice shooting at a target while the ball is still moving.

Making the Saves

To catch the ball, goalies form a "W" or a diamond shape with their thumbs and forefingers. This hand position prevents the ball from slipping between their hands and out of their control.

Goalies are both the last line of defense and the first line of attack for their team. They cover the penalty area and **save**, or stop, any balls that get past the defenders. After getting control of the ball, goalies start the next attack by passing the ball to a teammate. Goalies control the box, direct the defense, and warn of approaching attackers. They must be aware of what is happening during the game at all times.

Stand your ground

Move out into the penalty area to defend your net. It is harder to stop a shot if you are standing on the goal line. Take the **ready stance**—feet apart, knees bent, and hands raised—as the ball approaches. From this position, it is easier to react quickly to a shot. There are many ways to make a save. You can run, jump, or dive to catch the ball or punch or kick it away from the net. Try to stay on your feet so that you are ready for a **rebound**.

*Goalies **fist**, or punch, the ball away from the goal when they don't have enough time to catch it.*

Back on attack

After making a save, you should cradle the ball in both arms against your chest. Wait until all opponents have moved away from the goal area, then start your team's next attack—by rolling, throwing, or **punting** the ball to a teammate. You can take three steps before releasing the ball.

Tackling

*This girl is **block tackling** her opponent, which forces him to stop. She uses the inside of her foot to block the ball as he tries to dribble past her.*

Since a team can score only when it has possession of the ball, getting the ball away from opponents is an important skill to learn. This skill is called **ball collecting**. Members of a team on defense **tackle** attackers to get the ball from them. Players have to be careful when they tackle because it can accidentally turn into a **foul** (see pages 30-31)!

*A **poke tackle** is similar to a block tackle. Instead of stopping an opponent, however, it knocks the ball out of his or her control. To make a poke tackle, use your toes to poke the ball aside as your opponent is dribbling.*

Shoulder charge

A **shoulder charge** is the only type of touching allowed between soccer players. When running alongside an opponent, use your shoulder to bump his or her shoulder. The idea is only to knock the attacker off-balance so you can steal the ball—not to knock out your opponent! Keep your arms down while you charge so that you do not hit your opponent with your elbow.

Slide tackle

A **slide tackle** should only be used in desperation, when you are the last defender between an attacker and your goalie. Slide toward your opponent feet-first, and try to knock the ball out of control. Make sure you hit the ball—not your opponent!

You can practice your tackling skills with a friend. Set up a starting line and finish line and take turns being the tackler and attacker. The attacker has to dribble the ball from one line to the other without losing the ball to the tackler. It may help to have a third person to act as a referee.

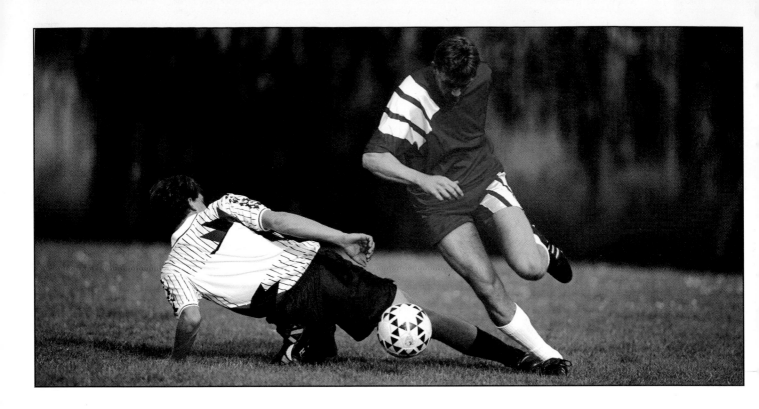

Playing by the Rules ⚽

(top) A slide tackle that touches the player instead of the ball can get you a major penalty. (above) The player on the right will get a minor penalty for hitting with his elbow.

Rules help keep the game fair and safe. When you foul, or break a rule, you get a **penalty**. The other team might then get control of the ball or get a chance to kick at the goal.

Foul!

There are two types of fouls—**major** and **minor**. Touching the ball with your hand or arm, tackling an opponent from behind, and purposefully kicking, tripping, or holding an opponent are major fouls. Minor fouls include blocking an opponent who doesn't have the ball, running at the goalie when he or she is holding the ball, and being **offside**.

Offside

The offside rule is meant to prevent players from waiting in front of their opponents' net. You are offside when you receive a pass in the other team's half of the field and there is only one opponent, such as the goalie, between you and the net.

offside

Free kicks

When you commit a foul the other team gets a **free kick**. The ball is placed on the ground where the foul occurred, and a player kicks it into play. If you commit a major foul, the other team gets a **direct free kick**—they can kick the ball directly at the goal. For a minor foul, an **indirect free kick** is given. The kicker must pass the ball to a teammate before a goal can be scored.

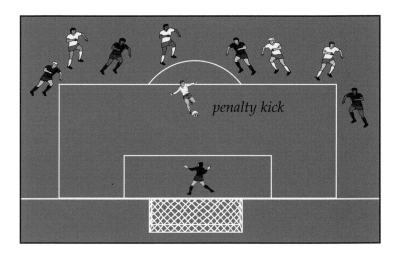

penalty kick

Penalty kicks

If you commit a major foul inside the penalty area, the other team gets a **penalty kick**. The ball is placed on the penalty spot, and one player kicks it at the goal. All other players must stand outside the penalty area and arc, and no one can move until the kicker touches the ball. Goals are often scored with penalty kicks.

*Referees have colored cards they can pull to show a penalty. A yellow card is a warning. A red card means the player is **ejected** from, or kicked out of, the game.*

Soccer Words

corner kick A free kick for the offensive team after the defending team puts the ball out-of-bounds over their own goal line. Corner kicks are taken from the corner circle nearest to the out-of-bounds play.

defender A player whose position is between the midfielders and the goalie to help protect the net

dribble To move the ball forward using short, quick kicks

FIFA (Fédération Internationale de Football Associations) The organization that regulates international soccer games

follow through To continue the kicking motion after the ball has been hit

forward A player who plays ahead of his or her teammates to lead attacks on the opponent's net

instep The top surface of the foot near the big toe

league An organized group of teams

midfielder A player whose position is between the defenders and forwards to help attack and defend

punt A kick made by the goalkeeper in which the ball is dropped from the hands and kicked into the air

rebound A ball that bounces off the goaltender or a goal post

referee The official who oversees the game to ensure it is played fairly

shin guard A thin protective pad that is worn underneath the sock

striker A forward who plays down the middle of the pitch

tackle A move used to get the ball away from an opponent

trap A move used to stop a ball and gain control of it

winger A forward who plays down the left or right side of the pitch

World Cup An international soccer tournament held by FIFA once every four years

Index

1 2 3 4 5 6 7 8 9 0 Printed in the U.S.A. 8 7 6 5 4 3 2 1 0 9